Naturally Sweet and Healthy Recipes for a Delicious Diet

Kory .Y Lowery

All rights reserved.

Copyright © 2024 Kory .Y Lowery

Naturally Sweet and Healthy Recipes for a Delicious Diet : Sugar-Free and Nutritious Meals to Fuel Your Body and Mind

Funny helpful tips:

Your actions echo in eternity; make choices that reflect the legacy you wish to leave.

Your essence is a gift; share it generously with the world.

<u>Life advices:</u>

Stay vigilant about deepfake technology; its ability to manipulate media poses challenges for authenticity verification.

Stay updated with advancements in photonic computing; leveraging light particles, it promises faster computational speeds.

Introduction

Within the pages of this book, you'll embark on a delicious journey into the world of guilt-free indulgence. In a realm where sweet treats often come with a hefty serving of sugar, this cookbook is a refreshing departure. It's your passport to a land of delectable desserts that not only satisfy your cravings but also align with a sugar-free lifestyle.

Indulging in dessert should never mean compromising on taste or health. That's precisely what this cookbook is all about. Whether you're following a sugar-free diet for health reasons, weight management, or simply seeking a more balanced way of life, you'll find a plethora of dessert options that cater to your needs.

From luscious cakes to tantalizing puddings, from chewy brownies to crispy cookies, this cookbook covers an extensive range of sugar-free delights. Each recipe is thoughtfully crafted to bring out the natural sweetness of ingredients like fruits, nuts, and spices, making every bite a guilt-free pleasure.

One of the standout features of this cookbook is its versatility. Whether you're an experienced baker or a novice in the kitchen, these recipes are designed to be accessible to everyone. You'll find step-by-step instructions, along with ingredient lists that are easy to follow, ensuring that your sugar-free creations turn out perfectly every time.

But this cookbook is more than just a collection of recipes; it's a celebration of flavors and textures that will delight your taste buds. You'll encounter classic favorites like chocolate cheesecake, banana bread, and chocolate chip cookies—all reimagined without the added sugar. Moreover, you'll discover innovative creations such as toasted Brazil nut truffles, cinnamon coconut chips, and avocado & melon salad, proving that sugar-free desserts can be both nutritious and tantalizing.

The inclusion of desserts and pudding recipes adds a touch of elegance to your culinary repertoire. Imagine savoring creamy rice pudding, raspberry & passion fruit swirl, or chocolate lava pots—all without the sugar crash afterward. With these recipes, you can enjoy dessert as an everyday delight or elevate it to a special occasion treat.

Additionally, this cookbook offers a variety of sweet treats, such as chocolate & bean fudge, peach & raspberry ice lollies, and sweet sugar-free popcorn. These options are perfect for satisfying cravings on the go, hosting gatherings, or simply enjoying a guilt-free snack whenever the mood strikes.

This book is more than just a cookbook; it's a testament to the belief that healthy eating and indulgence can coexist harmoniously. Whether you're seeking to maintain a sugar-free lifestyle or looking to reduce your sugar intake without sacrificing taste, this collection of recipes will become your trusted companion in the kitchen.

Get ready to embrace a world of sugar-free sweetness, where each dessert is a delightful discovery waiting to be shared with family and friends. With this cookbook in hand, you'll have the tools and inspiration to create an array of delectable desserts that prove sugar-free living can be not only enjoyable but also utterly delicious.

Contents

Recipes 1
Cakes 2
    Chocolate Cheesecake 3
    Pineapple Cream Cake 5
    Cinnamon & Walnut Mug Cake 6
    Strawberry & Lime MugCheesecake 7
    Vanilla Cupcakes 8
    Chocolate Cupcakes 9
    Orange Cream Cupcakes 10
    Banana Bread 12
    Black Forest Berry Cake 13
    Fresh Apricot Muffins 15
    Blueberry Breakfast Muffins 16
    Baked Chocolate OrangeCheesecake 17
    Low Carb Blueberry & AlmondCake 18
    Carrot Cake & Orange Icing 19
    Apple & Cinnamon Muffins 21
    Strawberry & Cream Scones 22
    Fruit Cake 23
    Quick Low-Carb RaspberryCheesecake 25
Brownies & Biscuits 26
    Raspberry & Chocolate Brownies 27
    Banana & Walnut Brownies 28
    Lemon Cheese Biscuits 29
    Banana Biscuits 30
    Peanut Butter Brownies 31
    Low Carb Chocolate Biscuits 33
    Double Choc Chip Cookies 34
    Pecan Nut & Cinnamon Biscuits 35
    Spiced Oat Biscuits 36

Fudgey Blackbean Brownies 37

Strawberry & Banana CookieBars 38

Ginger Biscuits 39

Vanilla Shortbread 40

Energy Balls & Healthy Snack Bars 41

Chocolate Red Velvet Bars 42

Chocolate Cashew Bars 44

Pumpkin Seed Bars 45

Coconut Protein Bars 46

Chocolate Dipped Quinoa Bars 47

Fresh Raspberry Protein Bars 48

Coconut & Cranberry Flapjacks 49

Cookie Dough Bars 50

Peanut Butter & BananaFlapjacks 51

Nutty Protein Balls 52

Chocolate Coconut & AlmondBars 53

Chocolate Balls 55

Chocolate Coated Almond Bars 56

Apple Pie Energy Bars 58

Chickpea & Chocolate ChipBlondies 59

Snowy Coconut Balls 60

Creamy Avocado ChocolateBites 61

Chilli Chocolate Bites 62

Desserts & Puddings 63

Banana & Blueberry Pudding 64

Creamy Rice Pudding 65

Raspberry & Passion Fruit Swirl 66

Apple & Walnut Creams 67

Ricotta Stuffed Peaches 68

Strawberry Fool 69

Rhubarb & Ginger Fool 70

Strawberry & Coconut Flan 71

Pecan & Apple Pie 73

Spiced Poached Peaches 74
Chocolate Mousse 75
Summer Pudding 76
Mango Ice Cream 77
'Real' Custard 78
Chocolate Lava Pots 79
Profiteroles 80
Chocolate Orange Ice Cream 82
Apple & Blackberry Pie 83
Rhubarb Crumble 85
Avocado & Melon Salad 86

Sweet Treats 87
Toasted Brazil Nut Truffles 88
Chocolate & Bean Fudge 89
Cinnamon Truffles 90
Peach & Raspberry Ice Lollies 91
Chocolate Crispie Cakes 92
Nut Brittle 93
Banana & Choc Chip Frozen Yogurt 94
Cherry Chocolate Milkshake 95
Tropical Ice Cream Lollies 96
Strawberry Jam 97
Sweet Sugar-Free Popcorn 98
Cinnamon Coconut Chips 99
Sweet Chilli Peanuts 100

Recipes

Cakes

Chocolate Cheesecake

Ingredients

For the base:
125g (4oz) butter
75g (3oz) ground almonds (almond meal/almond flour)
50g (2oz) pecan nuts
4 tablespoons 100% cocoa powder
3 teaspoons stevia powder (or to taste)
2 tablespoons coconut oil
2 large eggs
1 teaspoon vanilla extract

For the filling:
450g (1lb) ricotta cheese
4 teaspoons stevia sweetener
2 large eggs
1 teaspoon vanilla extract
60mls (2oz) double cream (heavy cream)

Serves 8-10

Method
Grease and line a spring form baking tin. Place the butter, coconut oil and cocoa powder into a saucepan and stir until the butter has melted. Remove it from the heat. In a bowl, combine the eggs, stevia and vanilla and mix well. Stir in the chocolate mixture, nuts

and ground almonds (almond flour/almond meal) and combine the ingredients. Spoon the mixture into the baking tin and press it into the edges. Transfer it to the oven and bake at 170C/325F for 15 minutes. Remove it and allow it to cool. In a bowl combine the ingredients for the filling and beat until smooth and creamy. Spread the filling over the top of the base. Transfer it to the oven and bake at 150C/300F for 40 minutes or until the cheesecake has completely set. Remove it from the oven and allow it to cool. Chill before serving.

Pineapple Cream Cake

Ingredients
For the base:
225g (8oz) ground almonds (almond flour/almond meal)
3 tablespoons coconut oil or vegetable oil
2 tablespoons water
Pinch of salt

For the filling:
450g (1lb) tinned crushed pineapple, in own juice (unsweetened)
Pinch of salt
1 teaspoon stevia sweetener (optional)
400mls (14fl oz) full-fat coconut milk

Serves 8

Method
Place the almonds, oil, water and salt into a bowl and combine them. Press the mixture into a spring form baking tin. Transfer it to the oven and bake at 170C/350F for 15 minutes. Allow it to cool. Pour the coconut milk into a food processor, add the pineapple and stevia and blend the ingredients together. Scoop the pineapple mixture on top of the base. Place it in the freezer until frozen. Defrost it before serving chilled.

Cinnamon & Walnut Mug Cake

Ingredients
2 teaspoons ground flaxseeds (linseeds)
2 tablespoons ground almonds (almond meal/almond flour)
1 tablespoon chopped walnuts
1 egg
½ teaspoon vanilla extract
½ teaspoon baking powder
½ teaspoon cinnamon
¼ teaspoon stevia (or to taste)
1 teaspoon coconut oil
Pinch of salt

Serves 1

Method
Place all the ingredients, except the walnuts, into a large mug or a microwaveable bowl and mix well. Cook in the microwave for 30 seconds, remove and stir then return it to the microwave for another 30 seconds, remove and stir in the walnuts. Return it to the microwave for another 30 seconds. Chill in the fridge before serving. Serve and enjoy.

Strawberry & Lime Mug Cheesecake

Ingredients
50g (2oz) cream cheese
25g (1oz) strawberries
2 tablespoons crème fraîche
1 egg
1 teaspoon lemon juice
½ teaspoon vanilla extract
½ teaspoon stevia extract (or to taste)

Serves 1

Method
Place all the ingredients, except the strawberries, into a large mug or a microwaveable bowl and mix well. Cook in the microwave for 30 seconds, remove and stir then return it to the microwave for another 30 seconds, remove and stir. Return it to the microwave for another 30 seconds. Chill in the fridge before serving. Serve with a scattering of strawberries

Vanilla Cupcakes

Ingredients
200g (7oz) butter
125g (4oz) self-raising flour
3 teaspoons stevia sweetener
2 large eggs
1 teaspoon vanilla extract

Makes 12

Method
Place the butter and stevia into a bowl and beat until smooth and creamy. Add the eggs and vanilla extract to the mixture and mix well. Sieve the flour into the wet mixture and combine. Place paper cases into a muffin tin and spoon some of the mixture into each one. Transfer to the oven, preheated to 180C/360F and bake for 10 minutes until slightly golden. Remove them and allow them to cool. This recipe for basic cupcake mixture can be livened up by adding unsweetened chocolate chips or topping them off with a swirl of cream cheese and a strawberry. Experiment and find your favourite.

Chocolate Cupcakes

Ingredients
125g (4oz) ground almonds (almond flour/almond meal)
2 eggs
2 tablespoons ground linseeds (flaxseeds)
1 tablespoon peanut butter or almond butter
1 tablespoon 100% cocoa powder
½ butternut squash, cooked and mashed
½ teaspoon bicarbonate of soda (baking soda)
60mls (2fl oz) coconut oil (melted)

Makes 6

Method
In a bowl, stir together the ground almonds (almond meal/almond flour), flaxseeds (linseeds) bicarbonate of soda and cocoa powder. Add the eggs to the mixture and combine. In a separate bowl, mix the squash, coconut oil and nut butter. Stir the squash mixture into the dry ingredients and mix well. Spoon the mixture into a 6 hole muffin tin and transfer to the oven. Bake at 180C/350F for 30 minutes. Test with a skewer which will come out clean when they're cooked.

Orange Cream Cupcakes

Ingredients

For the cupcakes:
175g (6oz) ground almonds (almond flour/almond meal)
75g (3oz) butter, softened
5 eggs, separated
4-5 teaspoons stevia sweetener (or to taste)
2 teaspoons baking powder
¼ teaspoon of cream of tartar
Zest of 1 orange
3 tablespoons orange juice

For the topping:
175g (6oz) cream cheese
4 teaspoons stevia sweetener

Makes 10 approx

Method
Place the ground almonds (almond flour/almond meal) and baking powder in a bowl and mix well. In a separate bowl combine the egg yolks, butter, orange juice and stevia and mix well. In a separate bowl whisk the egg whites together with the cream of tartar until if forms stiff peaks. Slowly fold the egg whites into the egg yolk mixture until gently combined. Fold in the almond mixture until well combined. Spoon the mixture into cupcake papers. Transfer to the

oven and bake at 180C/360F and cook for around 25 minutes. Test the cupcakes with a skewer which should come out clean. Allow them to cool. In a bowl, beat the cream cheese together with the stevia and orange zest and mix thoroughly. Spread some topping onto each of the cooled cupcakes.

Banana Bread

Ingredients
250g (9oz) plain flour (all-purpose flour)
125g (4oz) butter, softened
50g (2oz) walnuts, chopped (optional)
3 medium eggs
2 ripe bananas, mashed
2 teaspoons baking powder
1 teaspoon bicarbonate of soda (baking soda)
175mls (6fl oz) water

Serves 6

Method
Place the bananas and butter into a large bowl and combine them until the mixture is creamy. Add in the eggs and mix well. Add in the flour and bicarbonate of soda (baking soda) to the banana mixture. Slowly add in the water and beat the mixture well then stir in the walnuts (if using). Transfer the mixture into a greased baking tin. Transfer it to the oven, preheated to 180C/360F and cook for 35 minutes. Allow it to cool before cutting it into slices.

Black Forest Berry Cake

Ingredients
375g (13oz) plain flour (all-purpose flour)
250g (9oz) fresh mixed fruit (cherries, strawberries, blackberries, raspberries or blueberries)
175g (6oz) butter, softened
4-5 teaspoons stevia sweetener (or to taste)
2 teaspoons baking powder
250mls (8fl oz) freshly whipped cream
250mls (8fl oz) milk
3 eggs
1 teaspoon vanilla extract

Serves 12

Method
Place the flour, baking powder and stevia into a bowl and mix well. In a separate bowl combine the butter, eggs, milk and vanilla and beat until smooth and creamy. Fold the dry ingredients into the bowl of wet ingredients and combine them. Add in the fruit and mix well. Spoon the mixture equally into two baking tins. Transfer them to the oven and bake at 180C/360F and cook for around 25 minutes or until cooked through. Test the mixture using a skewer which should come out clean when it's done. Allow them to cool on a wire rack. Once completely cool, turn one cake upside down on a serving plate

and cover it in whipped cream. Place the other cake on top. Garnish with a swirl of cream and extra berries, if you wish.

Fresh Apricot Muffins

Ingredients
125g (4oz) coconut flour
100g (3 ½ oz) apricots, stone removed and chopped
3 eggs, whisked
2 ripe bananas, mashed
4 tablespoons coconut oil
1 teaspoon vanilla extract
½ teaspoon baking powder
Pinch of salt

Makes 12

Method
Place the eggs and bananas into a bowl and beat them until creamy. Place the coconut flour in a separate bowl and add in the baking powder, coconut oil, vanilla extract and a pinch of salt and mix well. Add in the egg mixture and combine until smooth. Add in the chopped apricots and mix well. Line a 12 muffin tin with paper cases and scoop some mixture into each one. Transfer them to the oven and bake at 200C/400F for 20 minutes or until cooked through and slightly golden.

Blueberry Breakfast Muffins

Ingredients
200g (7oz) wholemeal self-raising flour
175g (6oz) blueberries
50g (2oz) porridge oats
1 ½ teaspoons bicarbonate of soda (baking soda)
2-3 teaspoons stevia sweetener (or to taste)
2 ripe bananas, mashed
1 egg
100mls (3½fl oz) milk or almond milk

Makes 12

Method
Place the flour, oats, stevia and bicarbonate of soda (baking soda) into a bowl. In a separate bowl, mix together the mashed banana and egg. Add in the milk and mix well. Add the flour mixture into the wet mixture and mix well until there are no bits of flour or oats uncoated. Stir in the blueberries. Spoon the mixture into a 12-hole muffin tin. Transfer them to the oven and bake at 180C/360F for 20 minutes until slightly golden. Test the muffins with a skewer which should come out clean when they are cooked. Set them on a wire rack to cool.

Baked Chocolate Orange Cheesecake

Ingredients
800g (1¾ lb) cream cheese, such as mascarpone
4 eggs
4 tablespoons orange juice
3 tablespoons 100% cocoa powder
2 teaspoons stevia (or to taste)

Serves approx. 8

Method
Place all of the ingredients into a bowl and mix thoroughly. Transfer the mixture to a pie dish and bake at 170C/325F for one hour. Remove the cheesecake and allow it to cool. Chill before serving.

Low Carb Blueberry & Almond Cake

Ingredients
125g (4oz) ground almonds (almond meal/almond flour)
125g (4oz) blueberries (raspberries also work well)
4 medium eggs
2 teaspoons baking powder
2 teaspoons stevia powder (or to taste)
3 tablespoons olive oil
2 teaspoons vanilla extract

Serves 8

Method
Place the almonds, eggs, baking powder, stevia, oil and vanilla extract into a bowl and mix really well. Stir in the blueberries. Grease and line a small loaf tin with greaseproof paper. Transfer it to the oven and bake at 200C/400F for 20 minutes. This cake won't rise very much. Test it with a skewer which should come out clean. Allow to cool. Store in an airtight container.

Carrot Cake & Orange Icing

Ingredients
For the cake:
300g (11oz) carrots, grated (shredded)
150g (5oz) self-raising flour
100g (3½oz) ground almonds (almond meal/almond flour)
50g (2oz) walnuts, chopped
2 teaspoons ground mixed spice
3 eggs
3 teaspoons stevia powder
1 teaspoon bicarbonate of soda (baking soda)
100ml (3½fl oz) sunflower oil
3 tablespoons milk

For the icing:
150g (5) soft cheese
Grated zest of 1 orange

Serves 12

Method
Place the flour, walnuts, spice, bicarbonate of soda (baking soda) and stevia into a bowl and mix well. In a separate bowl, mix together the carrots, milk, eggs and oil. Pour the milk mixture into the flour mixture and combine well until thick and creamy. Grease and line a

baking tin with greaseproof paper. Pour the mixture into the baking tin and cook in the oven preheated to 180C/360F and cook for around 55 minutes. Test if it's cooked by using a skewer which should come out clean. Allow the cake to cool. Place it on a serving plate. In a bowl, mix together the orange zest and cream cheese. Spread the mixture onto the carrot cake. Slice, serve and enjoy.

Apple & Cinnamon Muffins

Ingredients
225g (8oz) apple, peeled and finely chopped
175g (6oz) plain flour (all-purpose flour)
100g (3½ oz) butter, softened
50g (2oz) ground almonds (almond meal/almond flour)
1 teaspoon bicarbonate of soda (baking soda)
2 teaspoons cream of tartar
1 teaspoon stevia sweetener (or to taste)
1 teaspoon ground cinnamon
2 eggs

Makes 12

Method
Place the butter and stevia sweetener into a food processor and blitz until smooth. Add in the ground almonds (almond meal/almond flour), flour, bicarbonate of soda (baking soda), cream of tartar, eggs and cinnamon and blitz until smooth. Add around ¾ of the apple and process. Stir in the remaining chopped apple. Transfer the mixture to a 12 hole muffin tin. Bake in the oven preheated to 180C/360F for 20 minutes. Test the muffins with a skewer which should come out clean. Allow them to cool. Store in an airtight container.

Strawberry & Cream Scones

Ingredients
250 (9oz) self-raising flour
2 teaspoons stevia sweetener
50g (2oz) butter
200mls (7fl oz) milk
For the topping:
150g (5oz) fresh ripe strawberries, chopped
250mls (8fl oz) double cream (heavy cream)

Makes 12

Method
Place the flour and stevia in a bowl and stir. Cut flakes of butter into the flour and using clean hands, rub it into the flour. Pour in the milk and mix to a dough. Grease and line a baking sheet. Scatter some flour onto a work surface and roll out the scone mixture to 2cm (1 inch) thick. Use a cookie cutter and cut into rounds. Place them onto the baking sheet and coat them with some extra milk. Transfer them to the oven, preheated to 180C/360F for around 20 minutes or until golden. Allow them to cool. Whisk the double cream (heavy cream) until thick. When ready to serve, cut the scones in half, dollop some cream on top and scatter chopped strawberries onto the cream. Enjoy!

Fruit Cake

Ingredients
250g (9oz) self-raising flour
200g (7oz) sultanas
75g (3oz) carrots, grated (shredded)
50g (2oz) dates, chopped
2 eggs
1 large apple, peeled, cored and chopped
1 teaspoon baking powder
½ teaspoon ground cinnamon
½ teaspoon ground nutmeg
250mls (8fl oz) hot water (for soaking)
100mls (3½ fl oz) vegetable oil

Serves 8

Method
Soak the sultanas and dates in a bowl of hot water for around 10 minutes. Drain off all the water. Grease and line a cake tin, around 18cm (7 inches) with greaseproof paper. Place the flour, baking powder, cinnamon, and nutmeg into a bowl and stir. Add in the eggs and oil and mix well. Stir in the apple, carrots, dates and sultanas. Pour the mixture into the prepared baking tin. Transfer it to the oven and bake at 180C/360F and cook for 45 minutes. Test the cake with

a skewer which should come out clean when it is completely cooked.

Quick Low-Carb Raspberry Cheesecake

Ingredients
200g (8oz) raspberries
200g (8oz) mascarpone cheese
75g (3oz) ground almonds (almond flour/almond meal)
1 tablespoon 100% cocoa powder

Serves 2

Method
Heat the raspberries in a saucepan until warmed through then set aside to cool. Sprinkle the ground almonds (almond flour/almond meal) onto the bottom of two serving bowls. Place the mascarpone cheese in a bowl, add in the cocoa powder and mix until smooth and well combined. Spoon the mixture on top of the almond base. Once the raspberries are cool, serve them on top. Enjoy.

Brownies & Biscuits

Raspberry & Chocolate Brownies

Ingredients
200g (7oz) self-raising flour (all-purpose flour)
100g (3½oz) butter
100g (3½oz) raspberries
50g (2oz) 100% cocoa powder
25g (1oz) cacao nibs or unsweetened chocolate chips
3 large free-range eggs, beaten
2 ripe bananas, mashed
1 teaspoon bicarbonate of soda
100mls (3½fl oz) milk

Makes approx. 16

Method
In a bowl, mix together the flour, cocoa powder and bicarbonate of soda (baking soda). Gently melt the butter in a saucepan, remove it from the heat and add in the bananas, milk and eggs and mix quickly. Pour the egg mixture into the flour mixture and mix thoroughly. Stir in the raspberries. Grease and line a baking tin with greaseproof paper. Scoop the brownie mixture into the baking tin. Scatter the cacao nibs/ chocolate chips over the mixture. Transfer it to the oven, preheated to 180C/360F and bake for around 30 minutes. Allow it to cool before cutting into squares.

Banana & Walnut Brownies

Ingredients
200g (7oz) self-raising flour
100g (3½oz) butter
50g (2oz) 100% cocoa powder
25g (1oz) walnuts, chopped
3 large eggs, beaten
3 ripe bananas, mashed
1 teaspoon bicarbonate of soda (baking soda)
100mls (3½fl oz) milk

Makes approx. 16

Method
In a bowl, mix the flour, cocoa powder and bicarbonate of soda (baking soda). Gently melt the butter in a saucepan, remove it from the heat and add in the bananas, milk and eggs and mix quickly. Pour the egg mixture into the dry ingredients and combine them thoroughly. Stir in the walnuts. Grease and line a baking tin with greaseproof paper. Spoon the mixture into the tin. Transfer it to the oven, preheated to 180C/360F and bake for around 30 minutes. Test it with a skewer which should come out clean when it's completely cooked. Allow it to cool before cutting into squares. These are delicious served warm with a dollop of cream.

Lemon Cheese Biscuits

Ingredients
75g (3oz) finely ground oats
50g (2oz) mascarpone cheese
3 teaspoons stevia powder (or to taste)
Zest and juice of ½ lemon
2 teaspoons vegetable oil
1 teaspoon vanilla extract

Makes 12

Method
Place the mascarpone in a bowl with the stevia, lemon zest, lemon juice, vanilla and vegetable oil. Stir in the oats and combine all of the ingredients until it becomes doughy. Scoop out spoonfuls of the mixture, shape them into balls and flatten them on a baking tray. Transfer them to the oven and bake at 170C/325F for 10 minutes. Allow to cool. Serve and enjoy.

Banana Biscuits

Ingredients
50g (2oz) butter, melted
50g (2oz) oats
50g (2oz) ground almonds (almond flour/almond meal)
25g (1oz) ground linseeds (flaxseeds)
2 ripe bananas
1 teaspoon vanilla extract

Makes 20

Method
Mash up the bananas in a large bowl and mix with the melted butter and vanilla. Add all of the remaining ingredients and combine. Leave to stand for 10 minutes and the mixture will firm up. Use a teaspoon to scoop out the dough. Roll it into balls and then pat down on a lined baking tray. Bake at 180C/360F for 15-20 minutes or until golden brown.

Peanut Butter Brownies

Ingredients
150g (5oz) ground almonds (almond meal/almond flour)
125g (4oz) butter
75g (3oz) smooth peanut butter
50g (2oz) 100% cocoa powder
50g (2 oz) coconut flour
50g (2oz) cacao nibs or unsweetened chocolate chips
2 large eggs
2 large egg yolks
2 teaspoons vanilla extract
3-4 teaspoons stevia sweetener (or to taste)
150mls (5fl oz) hot water
60mls (2fl oz) melted coconut oil

Makes 16

Method
In a bowl, whisk the hot water, cacao nibs and cocoa powder until the chocolate has melted. Stir in the butter and coconut oil, eggs and yolks, stevia and vanilla and whisk it well. Stir in the ground almonds (almond meal/almond flour) and coconut flour. Spoon the mixture into a square, greased and lined baking tin. Using the tip of a teaspoon, drop little blobs of peanut butter over the top of the mixture then using the tip of a skewer or knife make a swirly pattern

with the peanut butter. Transfer it to the oven and bake at 180C/360F and cook for 20 minutes. Allow to cool before cutting into squares. Store in an airtight container.

Low Carb Chocolate Biscuits

Ingredients
225g (8oz) tinned chickpeas (garbanzo beans)
125g (4oz) smooth peanut butter
3 tablespoons 100% cocoa powder
1 teaspoon vanilla extract
1 teaspoon stevia sweetener
1 teaspoon baking powder
200mls (7fl oz) soya milk or almond milk

Makes approx. 16

Method
Place all of the ingredients into a blender and process until smooth and creamy. If the mixture seems too thick try adding a little extra milk. Scoop out a spoonful of the mixture and place it on a greased baking tray. Repeat for the remaining mixture. Place it in the oven, preheated to 200C/400F and cook for 15 minutes.

Double Choc Chip Cookies

Ingredients
350g (12oz) plain flour (all-purpose flour)
250g (9oz) butter
100g (3 ½ oz) 100% cocoa powder
25g (1oz) cacao nibs or sugar-free chocolate chips
4 teaspoons stevia sweetener
2 eggs
1 teaspoon bicarbonate of soda (baking soda)

Makes approx. 20

Method
Place the butter and stevia powder in a bowl and mix until light and creamy. Add in the eggs and mix well. Sieve in the flour, cocoa powder and bicarbonate of soda (baking soda) and mix the ingredients for form a dough. Stir in the cacao nibs/chocolate chips. Dust a flat surface with flour and roll out the dough. Use a cooker cutter to cut it into the shapes. Grease a baking sheet and lay the biscuits onto it. Transfer to the oven and bake at 180C/360F for around 15 minutes or until golden. Allow to cool. Store in an airtight container.

Pecan Nut & Cinnamon Biscuits

Ingredients
125g (4½ oz) plain (all-purpose flour)
125g (4½ oz) butter
50g (2oz) pecan nuts
2 teaspoons stevia sweetener
1 teaspoon vanilla extract
1 egg, beaten
½ teaspoon bicarbonate of soda (baking powder)
½ teaspoon cinnamon

Makes approx. 16

Method
Place the flour, stevia, cinnamon and bicarbonate of soda (baking powder) into a bowl. Beat in the butter, vanilla extract and egg and mix until creamy. Stir in the pecan nuts. Line a baking sheet with greaseproof paper. Take out a spoonful of the mixture and using clean hands, roll it into balls. Place the balls on the baking sheet and press them down using the back of a spoon. Transfer them to the oven and bake at 180C/360F and cook for 10 minutes. Allow them to cool before serving.

Spiced Oat Biscuits

Ingredients
150g (5oz) butter
100g (3 ½ oz) rolled oats
4 teaspoons stevia sweetener
1 teaspoon ground allspice
Pinch of salt

Makes 10

Method
Place the butter and stevia into a saucepan a stir until melted. Place the oats, allspice and salt into a bowl and pour in the butter. Using clean hands, shape the mixture into balls. Grease a baking sheet and flatten the balls onto the baking sheet. Transfer to the oven and bake at 180C/360F for around 15 minutes or until the biscuits are golden. Remove them from the oven and allow them to cool. Store in an airtight container.

Fudgey Blackbean Brownies

Ingredients
400g (14oz) tin of black beans, rinsed and drained
75g (3oz) cocoa powder
50g (2oz) cacao nibs or dark chocolate chips
2 egg whites
1 large egg
1 ripe avocado
2-3 teaspoons stevia sweetener
¼ teaspoon cinnamon
¼ teaspoon bicarbonate of soda (baking powder)
¼ teaspoon salt
2 teaspoons vanilla extract
2 teaspoons olive oil

Makes 12

Method
Place all of the ingredients, except the cacao nibs/chocolate chips, into a blender and process until soft and smooth. If the mixture seems too thick, just add a teaspoon or two or water. Stir in the cacao nibs/ dark chocolate chips. Grease and line a baking tin and pour in the mixture. Transfer it to an oven preheated to 180C/360F for around 25 minutes. Allow it to cool before cutting into bars.

Strawberry & Banana Cookie Bars

Ingredients
3 medium-sized ripe bananas
150g (5oz) fresh strawberries, stalk removed and chopped
150g (5oz) plain flour (all-purpose flour)
100g (3 ½ oz) butter
3 ripe bananas
1 egg
1 teaspoon baking powder
1 teaspoon vanilla extract

Makes 12

Method
In a bowl, mash the bananas and then whisk in the egg. Melt the butter until it becomes liquid and add it to the banana mixture together with the vanilla extract. Stir in the strawberries. Sieve in the baking powder and flour and mix to a smooth dough. Transfer the mixture to a rectangular baking tin. Transfer to the oven, preheated to 180C/360F and cook for around 10 minutes or until golden. Allow it to cool. Cut into bars and store in an airtight container.

Ginger Biscuits

Ingredients
250g (9oz) plain flour (all-purpose flour)
150g (5oz) butter
2 teaspoons bicarbonate of soda (baking soda)
1 tablespoon ground ginger
1 teaspoon ground cinnamon
1 egg
Pinch of salt

Makes 12

Method
Place the flour, bicarbonate of soda, ginger, cinnamon and salt into a bowl and mix well. Heat the butter in a saucepan and allow to cool before beating the egg in with the butter. Slowly add the liquid to the dry ingredients. Grease a baking sheet and using clean hands, shape the mixture into balls. Flatten the balls into biscuit shapes on the baking sheet. Alternatively, roll out the mixture and using a cookie cutter, cut the dough into the required size. Transfer to the oven and bake at 180C/360F for around 10 minutes until golden. Allow them to cool. Remove and store in an airtight container.

Vanilla Shortbread

Ingredients
200g (7oz) plain flour (all-purpose flour)
150g (5oz) butter, softened
4 teaspoons stevia powder
2 teaspoons vanilla extract

Makes 8-10

Method
Place the butter, vanilla extract and stevia into a bowl and beat until light and creamy. Stir in the flour and mix to a dough. Dust a flat surface with a little flour and roll out the shortbread mixture to around 2cm (approx. 1 inch) thick. Use a cookie cutter to cut it into rounds. Grease a baking sheet and place the shortbread on the sheet. Transfer to the oven, preheated to 180C/360F and cook for around 20 minutes or until golden. Allow to cool before serving. You can even try adding chopped nuts or cacao nibs or cocoa powder to this recipe.

Energy Balls & Healthy Snack Bars

Chocolate Red Velvet Bars

Ingredients
250g (9oz) beetroot, peeled, boiled and allowed to cool
50g (2oz) coconut flour
50g (2oz) buckwheat flour
50g (2oz) cacao nibs or unsweetened chocolate chips
3 eggs
2 large ripe bananas, mashed
2 tablespoons 100% cocoa powder
1 teaspoon ground cinnamon
1 teaspoon bicarbonate of soda (baking soda)
2 tablespoons coconut oil, melted
2 teaspoons vanilla extract
Pinch of salt

For the topping:
50g (2oz) cacao nibs or unsweetened chocolate chips
1 teaspoon stevia sweetener

Makes 14

Method
Grease and line a baking tin then set it aside. Place the cooked beetroot into a food processor and blend to until smooth. Add in the eggs, banana, coconut oil and vanilla extract and combine them.

Place the coconut flour, buckwheat flour, cinnamon, bicarbonate of soda (baking soda) cocoa powder and cacao nibs/chocolate chips and a pinch of salt into a bowl and mix well. Stir in the beetroot and wet ingredients. Transfer the mixture to a baking tin and place it in the oven at 170C/325F for 30 minutes. Allow it to cool before cutting it into bars. Melt the cacao nibs/chocolate chips for the coating into a bowl over gently simmering water. Stir in the stevia sweetener and mix until completely melted. Drizzle the chocolate over the bars and allow them to cool. Store in an airtight container.

.

Chocolate Cashew Bars

Ingredients
125g (4oz) medjool dates
150g (5oz) unsalted cashews
50g (2oz) 100% cocoa powder
½ teaspoon peppermint extract
2 tablespoons almond milk
Pinch of salt

Makes 12

Method
Place all of the ingredients into a food processor and process until everything is well combined and a soft smooth texture. Spoon the mixture into a rectangular baking tin. Cover the mixture and chill it in the fridge for around 1 hours before cutting it into bars. Serve and eat straight away or stored them in an airtight container. If you wish to add extra protein to this recipe you can add a scoopful of your favourite protein powder to the ingredients.

Pumpkin Seed Bars

Ingredients
125g (4oz) almonds, roughly chopped
100g (3½oz) peanut butter
75g (3oz) pumpkin seeds, raw and unsalted
75g (3oz) sunflower seeds
50g (2oz) oats
50g (2oz) brazil nuts, roughly chopped
1 banana, mashed
1 teaspoon ground cinnamon
3 tablespoons raw honey
Pinch of sea salt

Makes 16

Method
Place the honey and peanut butter into a saucepan and gently warm it until it melts then remove it from the heat. Place the oats, almonds, brazil nuts, pumpkin seeds, sunflower seeds, cinnamon and salt into a bowl and mix well. Add the peanut butter mixture and banana into the dry ingredients and mix well. Grease and line a square baking tin with parchment paper. Spoon the mixture into the tin, pressing it into the edges. Transfer it to the oven and bake at 180C/360F for 15-20 minutes. Allow them to cool before cutting into bars. Enjoy.

Coconut Protein Bars

Ingredients
200g (8oz) desiccated coconut (shredded)
1 teaspoon vanilla extract
2-3 teaspoons stevia powder
4 tablespoons coconut oil
Pinch of salt

Makes 12

Method
Place all of the ingredients into a food processor and blitz until smooth. Line a square baking tin with parchment paper. Scoop the mixture into the tin and smooth it out to the corners. Transfer it to the fridge and chill for 1-2 hours. Cut it into 12 slices. Keep them in an airtight container in the fridge until ready to serve. As an alternative you can top the coconut bars with melted dark chocolate before they are ready to be chilled, making your very own bounty bars.

Chocolate Dipped Quinoa Bars

Ingredients
150g (5½ oz) quinoa, uncooked
150g (5½ oz) oats
125g (4 oz) peanut butter
100g (3½ oz) dark chocolate min (75% cacao)
3 teaspoons stevia sweetener

Makes approx. 20

Method
Scatter the oats and quinoa onto a baking sheet. Place it in the oven at 180C/360F for 7 minutes, stirring halfway through. Place the stevia and peanut butter into a bowl and microwave it until melted (or alternatively heat it in a saucepan). Place the oats and quinoa into a bowl and mix it well. Pour the peanut butter mixture into the dry ingredients and combine them. Grease and line a baking tin. Scoop the mixture into the baking tin, pressing it into the edges. Transfer it to the oven and bake at 180C/360F for 15-20 minutes. Remove them from the oven and allow them to cool before cutting into bars. Place the chocolate into a bowl and place it over a saucepan of gently simmering water until it melts. Dip each bar into dark chocolate then transfer them to the fridge. Enjoy.

Fresh Raspberry Protein Bars

Ingredients
125g (4oz) peanut butter
175g (6oz) oats
75g (3oz) raspberries
50g (2oz) linseeds (flaxseeds)
2 teaspoons stevia

Makes 12-14

Method
Place the oats, peanut butter, stevia and linseeds (flaxseeds) into a food processor and process until smooth. Stir in the raspberries. Spoon the mixture into a small baking tin and smooth it out. Chill in the fridge for 2 hours until the mixture has set. Cut it into bars and eat straight away or store them in the fridge. You could try substituting the raspberries for blueberries or chopped strawberries and unsweetened chocolate chips.

Coconut & Cranberry Flapjacks

Ingredients
200g (7oz) oats
50g (2oz) desiccated (shredded) coconut
50g (2oz) unsweetened dried cranberries
2 tablespoons almond butter
1 tablespoon coconut oil
2 teaspoons stevia sweetener
1 teaspoon vanilla extract

Makes 12

Method
Place the coconut oil, almond butter, stevia and vanilla extract into a saucepan and warm it gently whilst stirring. In a large bowl, mix together the oats and coconut. Pour the melted ingredients into the oats and combine them together. Add the cranberries and mix well. Grease and line a baking tin with greaseproof paper. Spoon the mixture into the baking tin and smooth it down. Transfer it to the oven and bake at 200C/400F for 12-14 minutes or until slightly golden. Allow it to cool before cutting into slices.

Cookie Dough Bars

Ingredients
100g (3½oz) oats
75g (3oz) almond nut butter
2 teaspoons vanilla extract
1-2 teaspoons stevia (optional)
150mls (5fl oz) almond milk

Makes 9

Method
Place the oats into a food processor and blitz until they become like flour. Add in the stevia (optional) and mix well. Add the almond butter, vanilla and half of the milk and pulse the mixture in the food processor. Gradually add in the remaining milk until it becomes a dough-like consistency. Grease and line a baking tray. Scoop the mixture into the baking tray and smooth it down. Cover and chill for at least 3 hours. Cut the mixture into bars. Serve and enjoy. For a variation to this recipe you can add some raw cocoa chips or drizzle with melted dark chocolate.

Peanut Butter & Banana Flapjacks

Ingredients
250g (9oz) rolled oats
3 tablespoons 100% cocoa powder
2 ripe bananas, mashed
2 tablespoons crunchy peanut butter
1 teaspoon ground cinnamon
Pinch of sea salt

Makes 8

Method
Place the oats, cocoa powder, cinnamon and salt into a bowl and mix well. Add in the mashed banana and peanut butter and combine all of the ingredients. Spoon the mixture into a shallow baking tin and press the mixture into the sides, smoothing it down. Cover and transfer it to the fridge to chill for 1 hour. Cut it into slices and serve.

Nutty Protein Balls

Ingredients
250g (9oz) ground almonds (almond flour/almond meal)
75g (3oz) desiccated (shredded) coconut
3 tablespoons chia seeds
4 tablespoons 100% cocoa powder
1 banana, mashed
1 tablespoon coconut oil
½ teaspoon vanilla extract
Pinch of salt

Makes 12

Method
Place the chia seeds in a large bowl with 2 tablespoons of water and let it sit for around 15 minutes until it thickens. Place the chia mixture into a bowl and add all of the other ingredients and combine them well until the mixture is well blended and thick. Using a teaspoon, scoop out the mixture and roll it in your (clean) hands to shape it into balls. Place the balls on a baking sheet and cook them at 190C/375F for 15 minutes.

Chocolate Coconut & Almond Bars

Ingredients
200g (7oz) desiccated (shredded) unsweetened coconut
200g (7oz) ground almonds (almond meal/almond flour)
1 large ripe banana
2 tablespoons melted coconut oil

For the topping:
100g (3½ oz) unsweetened chocolate chips or cacao nibs
Flesh of 1 large avocado
2-3 teaspoons stevia sweetener
2 teaspoons coconut oil
1 teaspoon vanilla extract

Makes 16

Method
Place the banana, coconut, coconut oil and almonds into a food processor and mix until soft. Grease and line a baking tin with parchment paper. Spoon the mixture into the tin and place it in the fridge to chill. Put the chocolate chips/cacao nibs into a bowl. Place the bowl over a saucepan of hot water and stir until they've melted. Place the avocado flesh, stevia, coconut oil and vanilla in the

blender and process until creamy. Pour the chocolate in and combine it with the avocado mixture. Once the base has chilled scoot the filling onto it and smooth it out. Cover and chill until completely set. Cut it into bars and keep it in the fridge until ready to serve.

Chocolate Balls

Ingredients
225g (8oz) chopped walnuts
150g (5oz) dates (pitted)
4 tablespoons 100% cocoa powder
2 tablespoons water
1 teaspoon vanilla extract
Pinch of salt
Extra cocoa powder for coating

Makes 12

Method
Place all of the ingredients into a food processor and mix until soft and creamy. Scoop out a spoonful of the mixture and using clean hands, shape it into a ball. Repeat for the remaining mixture. Sprinkle some cocoa powder onto a plate and roll the balls in it go give them a nice even chocolate dusting. Chill before serving.

Chocolate Coated Almond Bars

Ingredients
For the base:
200g (7oz) almonds
200g (7oz) desiccated (shredded) coconut
2 small ripe bananas
½ teaspoon sea salt
2 tablespoon coconut oil, melted

For the chocolate layer:
100g (3½ oz) dark chocolate (min 70 % cacao)
1 avocado
1-2 tablespoons stevia sweetener or to taste
1 teaspoon coconut oil
1 teaspoon vanilla extract

Makes 16

Method
Place the coconut and almonds into a food processor and blitz until they are finely ground. Add the banana, coconut oil and salt and combine until the mixture soft and doughy.
Line a baking tin with greaseproof paper and press the mixture into the tin, spreading it into the edges. Transfer it to the fridge to chill. In the meantime, place the chocolate into a bowl and place it over a

saucepan of gently simmering water until it melts. Place the avocado, stevia, coconut oil and vanilla in the blender and process until creamy. Pour the chocolate in and combine it with the avocado mixture. Take the chilled base mixture from the fridge and smooth on the chocolate topping. Cover the tin and return it to the fridge until the chocolate has set. Cut it into bars. Enjoy.

Apple Pie Energy Bars

Ingredients
175g (6oz) oats
125g (4oz) almond butter (or smooth peanut butter)
100g (3½oz) ground almonds (almond flour/almond meal)
3 large apples, peeled, cored and finely chopped
1 ½ teaspoons ground cinnamon
1 teaspoon ground mixed spice
1 teaspoon ground nutmeg
1-2 teaspoons stevia sweetener
5 tablespoons water

Makes 12

Method
Place the apples in a saucepan with five tablespoons of water. Gently warm the apples until they soften to a pulp then remove them from the heat and allow to cool. Place the oats, ground almonds (almond meal/almond flour) and spices in a large bowl and mix well. Place the almond butter and stevia together in a bowl and warm them in the microwave until it has melted. Combine the nut butter mixture with the dry ingredients and mix well. Add in the cooked apple and mix thoroughly. Line a baking tin and scoop the mixture into it, pressing it into the sides. Cover and chill for 30 minutes. Cut into slices and serve.

Chickpea & Chocolate Chip Blondies

Ingredients
400g (14oz) tin of chickpeas (garbanzo beans), drained
75g (3oz) smooth peanut butter or cashew butter
50g (2oz) unsweetened chocolate chips or cacao nibs
1 tablespoons raw honey
1 ripe banana
1 teaspoon vanilla extract
½ teaspoon bicarbonate of soda (baking soda)
100% cocoa powder for sprinkling (optional)

Makes 12

Method
Place all of the ingredients, apart from the cacao nibs/chocolate chips, into a food processor and mix until it becomes a smooth consistency. Stir in the chocolate chips. Grease and line a square baking tin and spoon the mixture into the tin. Transfer it to the oven and bake at 180C/360F for around 20 minutes. Test the mixture with a skewer which should come out clean when cooked. Sprinkle with cocoa powder (optional). Allow it to cool before cutting it into bars.

Snowy Coconut Balls

Ingredients
125g (4oz) almond butter
75g (3oz) macadamia nuts, chopped
75g (3oz) desiccated (shredded) coconut
2 tablespoons tahini paste
1 teaspoon vanilla extract
1 teaspoon stevia sweetener (or more to taste)
Extra coconut for coating

Makes 24

Method
Place the coconut, tahini, almond butter, vanilla extract and chopped macadamia nuts into a bowl and combine them thoroughly. Stir in a teaspoon of stevia powder then taste to check the sweetness. Add a little more sweetener if you wish. Roll the mixture into balls. Scatter some desiccated (shredded) coconut on a plate and coat the balls in it. Keep them refrigerated until ready to use.

Creamy Avocado Chocolate Bites

Ingredients
75g (6oz) dark chocolate, minimum 80% cocoa or cacao nibs
3 avocados, flesh removed
1 teaspoon vanilla extract
1 tablespoon honey (or ½ -1 teaspoon stevia powder) (optional)
100% cocoa powder for rolling
Pinch of salt

Makes approx. 14

Method
Place the chocolate in a large bowl and place it over a saucepan of gently simmering water until the chocolate has melted. Add in the vanilla, salt, honey or stevia (if using) and stir. Mash the avocado until it is smooth and creamy. Pour the melted chocolate into the avocado and mix it thoroughly. Chill in the fridge for 30 minutes until it becomes thicker. Using a teaspoon, scoop out the mixture and roll it into balls. Place the cocoa powder for rolling on a plate and completely coat the chocolate balls in the mixture. Serve and enjoy.

Chilli Chocolate Bites

Ingredients
125g (4oz) finely milled oats
50g (2oz) cacao nibs or unsweetened chocolate chips
3 teaspoons stevia powder (or to taste)
2 tablespoons 100% cocoa powder
1 teaspoon ground cinnamon
3 tablespoons coconut oil, melted
2 tablespoons water
1 teaspoon vanilla extract
¼ teaspoon cayenne pepper
Pinch of salt

Makes 16

Method
Place the oats, cayenne pepper, ground cinnamon, stevia, salt and cocoa powder into a bowl and mix well. Stir in the coconut oil, water and vanilla extract and combine all of the ingredients. Stir in the chocolate chips/cacao nibs. Grease and line a baking sheet. Scoop out a spoonful of the mixture, shape it into a ball and flatten it down on the baking sheet. Repeat for the remaining mixture. Place them in the oven and bake at 170C/325F for 12 minutes. Allow them to cool before serving.

Desserts & Puddings

Banana & Blueberry Pudding

Ingredients
150g (5oz) risotto rice
100g (3½ oz) fresh blueberries
1 large ripe banana
1 vanilla pod, cut open
1 litre (1¾ pints) almond milk

Serves 4

Method
Pour the almond milk into saucepan and add the rice, banana and vanilla pod. Bring it to the boil then reduce the heat and simmer for 15 minutes until the rice is cooked through and soft. Remove the vanilla pod and stir in the blueberries. Serve the pudding immediately.

Creamy Rice Pudding

Ingredients
125g (4oz) risotto rice
50g (2oz) hazelnuts, chopped
50g (2oz) almonds, chopped
50g (2oz) butter
2 teaspoons stevia sweetener
1 teaspoon ground cinnamon
600mls (1 pint) warm milk

Serves 4

Method
Heat a frying pan, add the chopped nuts and toast until golden, then set aside. Heat the butter in a saucepan, stir in the rice and cook for around 1 minute. Slowly add the warm milk to the rice, stirring continuously. Add the stevia and cinnamon and simmer gently for around 20 minutes until the rice is soft. Serve the rice pudding into bowls and sprinkle with the toasted nuts.

Raspberry & Passion Fruit Swirl

Ingredients
400g (14oz) mascarpone cheese
275g (10oz) raspberries
Seeds of 2 passion fruit
A few extra raspberries to garnish

Serves 4

Method
Place the raspberries in a bowl and mash them to a pulp. In a separate bowl, stir the seeds from the passion fruit into the mascarpone and mix well. Take decorative glasses or dessert bowls and spoon a layer of the mascarpone in then add a spoonful of the raspberry purée and swirl it slightly, repeat with another layer of mascarpone and raspberry until the mixture has been used up. Garnish with a few raspberries and chill before serving.

Apple & Walnut Creams

Ingredients
100g (3½ oz) cream cheese
50g (2oz) walnuts, roughly chopped
4 apples
½ teaspoon ground cinnamon
3 tablespoons lemon juice

Serves 4

Method
Peel and core the apples then slice them evenly width ways to create a circular shape. Lightly coat the apple slices in lemon juice and place them on a serving plate. Mix together the cream cheese, cinnamon and walnuts then spoon a little of the mixture onto each apple ring. Eat immediately.

Ricotta Stuffed Peaches

Ingredients
100g (3½ oz) ricotta
4 large ripe peaches, halved and stone removed
2 tablespoons oat bran
Zest and juice of 1 orange

Serves 4

Method
Place the peaches in an oven-proof dish with the flat side facing up. Place the orange zest and juice, oat bran and ricotta cheese into a bowl and combine the ingredients. Spoon the creamy mixture into the centre of the peaches. Bake them in the oven at 180C/360F for 15 minutes. Serve them on their own or with a little crème fraîche or plain yogurt.

Strawberry Fool

Ingredients
350g (12oz) strawberries
175mls (6fl oz) plain unflavoured yogurt
175mls (6fl oz) whipping cream (heavy cream) or crème fraîche
1 teaspoon stevia (optional)
A few extra strawberries to garnish

Serves 4

Method
Place the strawberries into a blender and puree them. If you require extra sweetness mix in the stevia powder. Push the strawberry purée through a sieve to remove all of the seeds. Whip the cream until thick then combine it with the yogurt. Mix the strawberry purée with the cream and yogurt. Spoon the dessert into decorative glasses and top with a few strawberries. Chill before serving.

Rhubarb & Ginger Fool

Ingredients
450g (1lb) rhubarb, thickly chopped
150g (5oz) Greek yoghurt
3 teaspoons stevia sweetener
1 teaspoon ground cinnamon
1 teaspoon ground ginger
50mls (2fl oz) freshly squeezed orange juice

Serves 6

Method
Place the orange juice, rhubarb, cinnamon, ginger and stevia into a saucepan and cook for 10-15 minutes until the rhubarb has softened. Remove from the heat and allow it to cool. Swirl the yogurt into the rhubarb mixture. Spoon it into dessert bowls or glasses and chill before serving.

Strawberry & Coconut Flan

Ingredients

For the base:
100g (3½oz) hazelnuts
100g (3½ oz) cashew nuts
3 teaspoons stevia sweetener
2 teaspoons water
1 teaspoon vanilla extract

For the topping:
175g (6oz) ripe strawberries
100g cashew nuts
50g (2oz) desiccated coconut
4 teaspoons stevia sweetener
75g (3oz) coconut oil, melted
1 teaspoon vanilla extract
A few strawberries to garnish

Serves 10

Method
Place the nuts and stevia into a blender and process until soft and smooth. Add in the vanilla extract and water and mix until it begins to stick together. Transfer the mixture to a flan tin and place it in the

fridge for 45 minutes to allow it to firm up. Place the cashew nuts, strawberries, desiccated coconut, coconut oil, stevia and vanilla extract into a food processor and mix until smooth. Spoon the strawberry mixture onto the flan base. Chill in the fridge for at least an hour and serve with a few strawberries scattered on top.

Pecan & Apple Pie

Ingredients
250g (9oz) pecan nuts
8 apples, peeled, cored and finely sliced
1 ½ teaspoons ground cinnamon
1 tablespoon butter
1 teaspoon vanilla extract
2 tablespoons water
Pinch of salt

Serves 6

Method
Place the nuts, cinnamon, butter, vanilla, salt and water into a food processor and blitz until smooth. Spoon the mixture into a pie dish and smooth it down. Transfer it to the oven and bake at 190C/375F for around 10 minutes. Remove it from the oven. Cover the base with the apple slices and a sprinkling of cinnamon (optional). Reduce the oven temperature to 180C/360F. Cover the pie with foil, place it in the oven and cook for around 45 minutes. Serve with a dollop of whipped cream or crème fraîche. Enjoy.

Spiced Poached Peaches

Ingredients
4 star anise
4 large peaches
2 cinnamon sticks
300mls (½ pint) water
2 teaspoons stevia sweetener

Serves 4

Method
Place the stevia and water in a saucepan and bring to the boil. Add the peaches, star anise and cinnamon sticks. Reduce the heat and simmer gently for 10 minutes. Remove the peaches, cover to keep them warm and set aside. Continue cooking the liquid for another 5 minutes. Serve the peaches with the liquid drizzled over the top.

Chocolate Mousse

Ingredients
150mls (6fl oz) double cream (heavy cream)
100g (3½ oz) cream cheese such as mascarpone or ricotta
2 tablespoons butter
2 tablespoons 100% cocoa powder
2 teaspoon stevia (or to taste)

Serves 4

Method
Place the butter and stevia into a bowl and mix well. Stir in the cream cheese and cocoa powder and mix thoroughly. Whip the cream until thick and fold it into the mixture. Spoon the mousse into dessert bowls and chill before serving.

Summer Pudding

Ingredients
450g (1lb) strawberries, stalks removed
450g (1lb) raspberries
2 teaspoons stevia sweetener (optional)
6 slices of thick bread

Serves 6-8

Method
Place the strawberries and raspberries into a saucepan, together with the stevia (if using) and heat gently until the fruit has softened. Remove and set aside.

Using a large bowl, place the bread slices around the bowl, completely lining it so that there are no gaps. You may need to slice the bread into smaller pieces to make it fit. Spoon the fruit into the bowl. Place a plate that fits just inside the bowl and press it down. Place it in the fridge for around 1 hour making sure it is completely chilled before turning out and serving. Serve with a dollop of cream.

Mango Ice Cream

Ingredients
3 ripe mangoes, de-stoned and peeled
600mls (1 pint) double cream (heavy cream)
Juice of 1 lime

Serves 6

Method
Place the mango into a food processor and blitz until smooth. Add in the cream and lime juice and process until smooth and creamy. Transfer the mixture to an airtight container and place it in the freezer. Whisk with a fork after 1-2 hours and continue to freeze. Alternatively pour the mixture into an ice cream maker and follow the manufacturer's instructions.

'Real' Custard

Ingredients
4 egg yolks
1 egg
1 tablespoon stevia sweetener
1 teaspoon vanilla extract
1 teaspoon cornflour
600mls (1 pint) full fat milk
100mls (3½fl oz) double cream (heavy cream)

Serves 4

Method
Take a large bowl and beat your egg yolks and egg. Add your stevia sweetener and cornflour and mix well. Pour the milk into a saucepan along with the vanilla extract. Bring it to the boil. Slowly add the hot milk to the egg mixture and stir well. Pour back into a large pan with your cream and stir until thickened. Enjoy with a hot or cold dessert.

Chocolate Lava Pots

Ingredients
100g (3½oz) cacao nibs or 85% cocoa chocolate
50g (2oz) butter
25g (1oz) coconut flour
2 large eggs (beaten)
2 teaspoons stevia
25mls (1floz) milk

Serves 2

Method
Grease 2 ramekin dishes with a little butter. Place the chocolate, stevia and butter in a bowl and place it over a saucepan of gently simmering water. Place the coconut flour in a bowl and stir in the beaten eggs. Warm the milk to just before it starts to simmer. Slowly pour the milk into the egg mixture and whisk continuously. Stir the chocolate mixture into the flour mixture. Spoon the mixture into the ramekin dishes. Transfer them to the oven and cook at 200C/400F for 12-14 minutes. Serve and eat straight away. The centre should be liquid chocolate. Enjoy.

Profiteroles

Ingredients

For the profiterole:
75g (3oz) plain flour (all-purpose flour), sieved
50g (2oz) butter (unsalted)
2 teaspoons stevia sweetener
2 eggs, beaten
60mls (2fl oz) cold water

For the filling:
250mls (8fl oz) whipping cream
1 teaspoon vanilla extract
1 teaspoon stevia sweetener (optional)

For the chocolate topping:
2 tablespoons 100% cocoa powder
2 teaspoons stevia sweetener (or to taste)
60mls (2fl oz) double cream (heavy cream)
1 teaspoon vanilla extract

Makes approx. 20

Method
Place the flour in a bowl with the stevia sweetener, mix and set aside. Place the water and butter in a saucepan, bring it to the boil and remove from the heat. Whisk in the flour, until it forms a thick paste. Add the egg, stirring constantly until smooth. Scoop out the

mixture using a teaspoon and place them onto a baking tray lined with parchment paper until you've used up all of the mixture. Transfer to the oven and bake at 200C/400F and cook for 10 minutes, then increase the temperature to 220C/440F and cook for another 5 minutes. Prick each profiterole with a thin skewer to let the moisture out and allow them to cool completely. Whisk up the cream, vanilla extract and stevia (if using) and set aside. Place the cream, cocoa powder, stevia and vanilla extract into a saucepan and warm it gently, stirring constantly. Set aside for it to cool down. Cut each profiterole almost in half, place a teaspoon of cream into it and replace the lid. Coat each profiterole in some of the sauce. Serve and eat immediately.

Chocolate Orange Ice Cream

Ingredients
200g (8oz) 100% cocoa powder
3 teaspoons stevia powder
Zest and juice of 2 oranges
600mls (1 pint) double cream (heavy cream)

Serves 6

Method
Place the cocoa powder and stevia in a bowl and stir in the cream. Add in the orange zest and juice and mix thoroughly. Transfer the mixture to an ice-cream maker and follow the manufacturer's instructions. Alternatively, pour the mixture into an airtight container and place it in the freezer. Whisk it with a fork after freezing for around an hour then return it to the freezer once more.

Apple & Blackberry Pie

Ingredients

For the pie crust:
400g (14oz) plain flour (all-purpose flour)
200g (7oz) butter or margarine
1 tablespoon water

For the filling:
250g (9oz) blackberries
250g (9oz) sweet apples
2-3 teaspoons stevia sweetener (optional if the fruit is very sweet)
1 teaspoon ground cinnamon
½ teaspoon ground nutmeg
125mls (4fl oz) warm water

Serves 8

Method

Place the flour into a bowl, add the butter and using clean fingers, rub the flour into the butter until it is partially bound together. Stir in the water to bind the pastry together. Roll out half of the pastry onto a floured surface. Grease a pie dish and place the pastry over the dish, trimming any excess from around the dish. Bake the pastry blind in an oven preheated to 200C/400F for 5 minutes. In the meantime, place the blackberries, apples, cinnamon, nutmeg and stevia (if using) into a saucepan and pour in the water. Cook for around 5 minutes, stirring occasionally. Scoop the filling into the prepared pie crust. Roll out the rest of the pastry, cover the filling and trim off any excess. Place the pie in the oven and cook for around 20 minutes or until slightly golden. Serve with sugar-free 'real' custard or cream.

Rhubarb Crumble

Ingredients

For the filling

675g (1½ lb) fresh rhubarb, leaves removed and chopped
3 teaspoons stevia sweetener (or to taste)

For the crumble:

100g (3½oz) plain flour (all-purpose flour)
100g (3½oz) butter
2 teaspoons stevia sweetener

Serves 6

Method

Place the rhubarb into a saucepan and pour in just enough water to cover it. Bring it to the boil, reduce the heat and simmer for 5 minutes until it begins to soften. Stir in 3 teaspoons of stevia and set aside.

Place the flour in a bowl and stevia into a bowl and stir. Rub in the butter until it becomes crumbly. Spoon the rhubarb into a large ovenproof dish and scatter the crumble over the top. Transfer it to the oven, preheated to 200C/400F and cook for around 15 minutes or until golden. Remove it from the oven and serve it with a swirl of cream. Delicious!

Avocado & Melon Salad

Ingredients
2 large ripe avocados, sliced
1 cantaloupe melon, cubed
½ teaspoon ground ginger
Juice of 1 lemon

Serves 4

Method
Mix the lemon juice and ginger together in a bowl. Add the avocados and melon and toss gently. Chill before serving.

Sweet Treats

Toasted Brazil Nut Truffles

Ingredients
200g (7oz) toasted coconut flakes
100g (3½oz) Brazil nuts, chopped
2 teaspoons vanilla extract
2 tablespoons coconut oil

Serves 4

Method
Place all of the ingredients into a blender and process until smooth and creamy. Add a little extra coconut oil if required. Divide the mixture into bite-size pieces and roll it into balls. Place the balls into small paper cake cases. Chill before serving.

Chocolate & Bean Fudge

Ingredients
400g (14oz) tin of black beans, rinsed and drained
75g (3oz) 100% cocoa powder
50g (2oz) cacao nibs or unsweetened chocolate chips
2 egg whites
Flesh of 1 ripe avocado
1 large egg
½ teaspoon bicarbonate of soda (baking soda)
2 teaspoons vanilla extract
3 teaspoons stevia sweetener
1 teaspoon coconut oil

Makes approx. 12

Method
Place all of the ingredients, except the cacao nibs/chocolate chips, into a blender and process until soft and smooth. Stir in the cacao nibs/chocolate chips. Grease and line a baking tin with parchment paper. Spoon the mixture into the tin. Transfer it to the oven and bake at 180C/360F for around 25 minutes. Allow the fudge to cool. Cut it into squares. Store in an airtight container until ready to use.

Cinnamon Truffles

Ingredients
150g (6oz) hazelnuts
100g (3½oz) pitted dates
25g (1oz) desiccated (shredded) unsweetened coconut
3 tablespoons 100% cocoa powder
1 teaspoon ground cinnamon
½ teaspoon ground ginger
1 tablespoon coconut oil
1-2 tablespoons water (optional)

Makes 14

Method
Place the nuts into a food processor and blend until they become fine. Add in the remaining ingredients and blitz them until soft and sticky. Try adding a spoonful or two of water if the mixture seems too thick. Using clean hands, shape the mixture into balls. Chill before serving.

Peach & Raspberry Ice Lollies

Ingredients
4 ripe peaches, de-stoned
8 raspberries, halved
1 banana, peeled
1 teaspoon lemon juice

Serves 6

Method
Gently drop the peaches in a saucepan of hot water and remove after around 20 seconds and place them into a bowl of cold water. Remove the skin from the peaches which will have now loosened. Place the peaches, banana and lemon juice in a blender and blitz until smooth. Stir in the raspberries pieces. Pour the mixture into ice lolly moulds and insert the sticks. Transfer to the freezer until set.

Chocolate Crispie Cakes

Ingredients
150g (5oz) rice puffs (sugar-free)
100g (3½oz) 100% cocoa powder
3 tablespoons butter
3 teaspoons stevia powder (or to taste)

Method
Place the butter and stevia into a saucepan and warm it until it melts. Stir in the cocoa powder and mix thoroughly. Add the rice puffs to the chocolate and coat them completely. Spoon the mixture into individual cupcake papers. Allow to cool before serving.

Nut Brittle

Ingredients
175g (6oz) 100% cocoa powder
25g (1oz) butter
25g (1oz) whole hazelnuts
25g (1oz) Brazil nuts
3 teaspoons stevia powder (or to taste)

Serves 4

Method
Place the butter in a saucepan along with the stevia and stir until melted. Stir in the cocoa powder and mix well. Stir in the nuts and mix well to coat them completely. Spread the nuts on a greased baking sheet. Transfer it to the fridge and chill for around 1 hour or until set. Chop it into rough chunks. Enjoy.

Banana & Choc Chip Frozen Yogurt

Ingredients
900g (2lb) plain Greek yogurt
50g (2oz) cacao nibs or unsweetened chocolate chips
4 large ripe bananas
4 teaspoons stevia powder
1 teaspoon vanilla extract

Serves 6-8

Method
Place the bananas, yogurt, stevia and vanilla extract into a food processor and mix until smooth and creamy. Stir in the cacao nibs/unsweetened chocolate chips. Transfer the mixture to an ice cream maker and freeze the yogurt according to the manufacturer's instructions. Alternatively, pour the yogurt into a container and freeze it for one hour. Remove it and whisk with a fork. Return it to the freezer and whisk again after another hour and continue until completely set. Serve and enjoy.

Cherry Chocolate Milkshake

Ingredients
Flesh of ½ avocado
75g (3oz) frozen cherries
1 tablespoon 100% cocoa powder
100mls (3½fl oz) milk or almond milk

Serves 1

Method
Place all of the ingredients into a food processor and blitz until smooth and creamy. Pour it into a tall glass and serve.

Tropical Ice Cream Lollies

Ingredients
1 pineapple, peeled and chopped
200mls (7fl oz) coconut milk

Makes approx. 12

Method
Place the pineapple and coconut into a food processor and process until it's really smooth and creamy. Pour the mixture into ice lolly moulds. Place them in the freezer until completely set. Keep in the freezer until ready to use.

Strawberry Jam

Ingredients
375g (13oz) strawberries, stalk removed
25g (1oz) chia seeds
4 teaspoons stevia sweetener

Method
Place the strawberries into a food processor and blitz until smooth. Place the strawberries to a bowl and stir in the stevia and chia seeds and mix well. Cover the bowl and place it in the fridge for 2 ½ hours. Spoon the strawberry mixture into a food processor and mix until jam-like. Transfer the mixture to a clean jam-jar and cover it. Store the jam in the fridge.

Sweet Sugar-Free Popcorn

Ingredients
100g (3½oz) unpopped popcorn
2 teaspoons butter or coconut oil
1 teaspoon stevia sweetener

Method
Place the butter/oil and stevia into a large saucepan and gently warm it while stirring. Turn the heat up high. Add the uncooked popcorn and place a lid on the saucepan. Cook for around 2-3 minutes or until all the corn has popped. Allow it to cool before serving.

Cinnamon Coconut Chips

Ingredients
175g (6oz) unsweetened coconut flakes
1 teaspoon cinnamon
½ teaspoon stevia sweetener (optional)

Serves 4

Method
Scatter the coconut flakes onto a baking sheet. Sprinkle the cinnamon and stevia (if using) over the coconut. Transfer them to the oven and cook at 170C/325F for around 5 minutes until the coconut is slightly golden. Allow them to cool. Serve and enjoy.

Sweet Chilli Peanuts

Ingredients
275g (10oz) unsalted peanuts
25g (1oz) butter
2 teaspoons stevia sweetener
½ teaspoon cayenne pepper
Pinch of salt

Serves 4-6

Method
Place the butter in a bowl and beat in the stevia, cayenne pepper and salt. Line a baking sheet with greaseproof paper. Stir the peanuts into the butter mixture and coat them well. Spread them onto the baking sheet. Transfer them to the oven and cook at 180C/360F and roast them for 10 minutes, giving them a stir halfway through. Allow them to cool before serving.

Printed by Amazon Italia Logistica S.r.l.
Torrazza Piemonte (TO), Italy